A Few Haikus

A Few Haikus:

3 little lines from the modern mind

Kelsey Cavalli

ISBN: 9798218328856

First Printing, 2023

Cover Design by Kelsey Cavalli

Dedicated to all the dreamers, the lovers, the visionaries, the creatives:

This book was written not with the intention of being the best writer or the most popular or successful, but to ignite, fuel, and inspire any ounce of creativity you may have towards making your dreams a reality. I wanted this book to serve as tangible proof that anything you ever wanted to achieve, you can. My only hope is that the significance of this book is not measured by its content or literal context, but by its symbolic representation of a dream turned into a reality, which I hope motivates you to pursue as well. This is your wake-up call to keep dreaming, dream big, take a chance, and never let anyone dim your shine!

Rather than just being a literal book, I wanted this piece to symbolize the actual physical manifestation of an idea materialized into reality. From thoughts turned to paper, it's now something I can hold and cherish. I hope this symbolic statement ignites a passion in you to create, to aspire, to dream.

Orbiting away,

Waxing and waning through you;

...We're elliptical

A cookie cutter

Made of a different mold-

A new type of treat.

I've stopped pretending;

No more masks to hide behind—

It's time to be free!

Beautiful flowers,

Take care of them and they grow.

Neglect them, they die

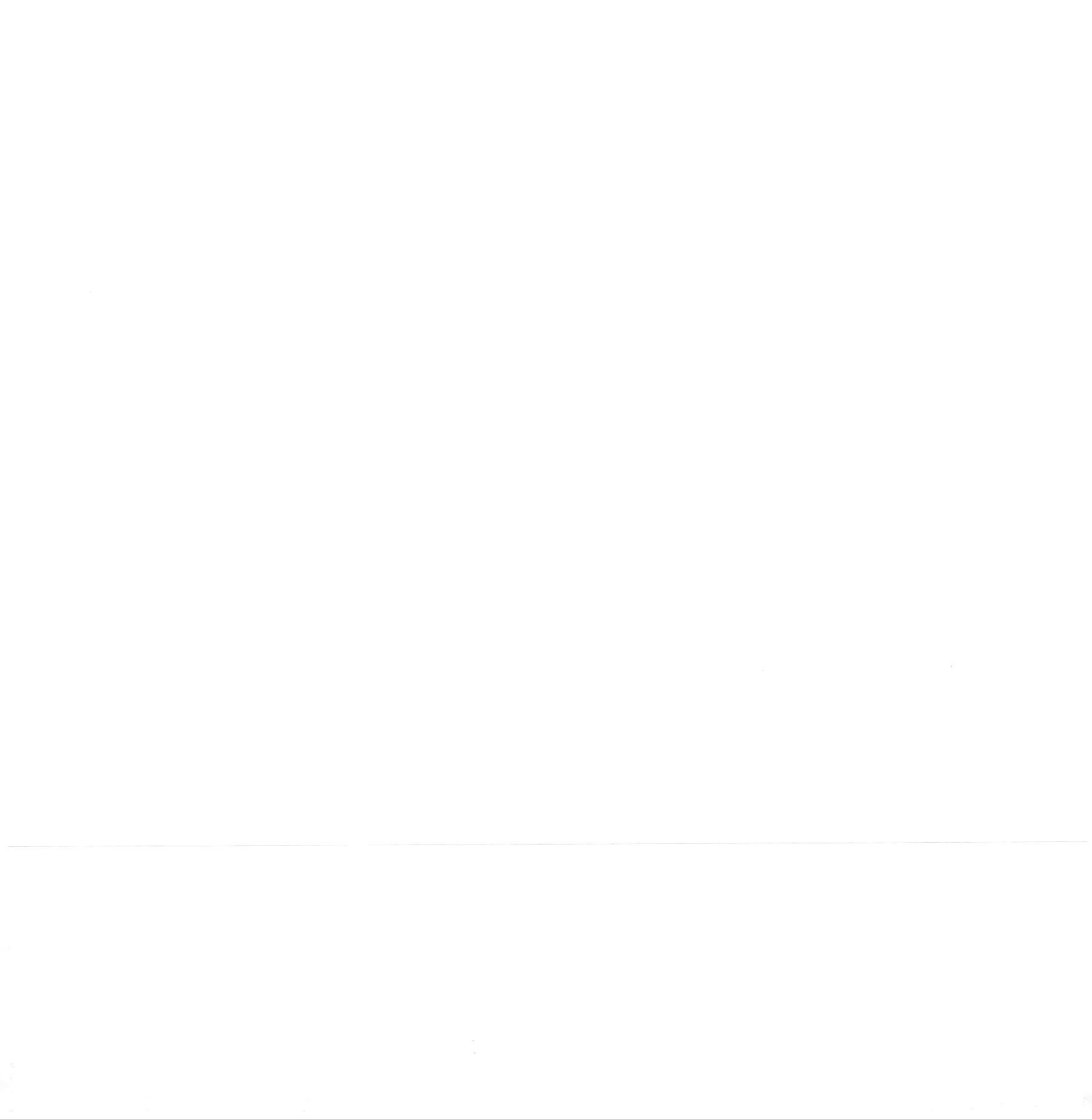

Completely unhinged,

It's my time to shine bright now;

Hell hath no fury

Trembling, rolling;

Like sounds of distant thunder,

Crashing into me

I change, and evolve-

Just like as the seasons do;

I've changed.

Self-built from pressure,

Apply it & watch me shine;

Cut like a diamond.

Don't give up just yet;

When the sun rises you'll find

You have made it through

Under a big stone,

I am hiding forever;

An introvert's dream

I just want to say,

If you'd please let me finish-

Stop cutting me off!

Soulmates forever?

A once eternal promise,

Now gone with the wind.

Hang on and be brave;

For those who need to hear this

Having a rough day

Just two souls in the void

Ebbing and flowing in space;

But in you, I'm found.

Miles in between us,

But not even the distance

Can alter our fate

With my red dress on,

The devil caught me dancing-

With another man.

How lonely it feels;

You're sitting right next to me

But feel worlds away…

Silent night descends,

Witching hour draws ever near;

Spells and magic rise

Not even hellfire,

Nor dark threats of despair can

Silence a thorned rose.

Sky turns golden red,

Sun descends in quietness,

Peaceful rest ahead.

Dimensions away,

Stretched across the universe;

I would still find you

In the dark unknown,

Alien mystery abounds,

Secrets yet untold.

In the beginning

There was only darkness...

And then came the light

Heart racing, mind spins-

Heavy weight on shoulders sinks;

A n x i e t y grips.

Twisted strands of life

Encoded instructions within-

DNA, our code.

You're here next to me

But there's miles in between us-

So close, but so far

Heart pounding, chest tight

Breath quickens, thoughts take flight

Choking on panic

Blessed drops divine,

Holy water purifies,

Soothes and saves my soul

Inbox overflowing,

Too many emails to read,

Time to hit delete.

Vodka starts to hit-

One night of wild temptation,

Brings morning regret.

Racing down the street

Missed my train and clock's ticking;

Late for work again!

Soft sanctuary;

A cozy retreat awaits-

My bed, solace found.

Empty pockets ache,

Debts and bills start to pile up,

I hate being broke.

Passionate embrace,

Two hearts beating as one soul,

Symbiotic flames.

Do you, dear sister!

With grace and strength in your heart,

Light up the world's dark!

Tequila regrets;

Morning after blues set in-

Never again, friend.

I don't want to get

Caught up in worries and stress-

Peace, I long to find

Uber ride cancelled

Left standing in the rainstorm,

Frustration sets in.

Boss bitch in the lead

Powerful and confident,

Success is her game

Euphoric feeling,

High on life, soaring above,

Endless possibilities

Insecurities rise

Like a storm cloud in the sky,

Thunder in my heart

Winter's chill sets in,

Frozen heart yearns for warmth's touch,

Spring thaw brings new life.

In bed I find peace,

Under the cozy covers.

5 more minutes please!

Our whole existence,

A weird and wonderful world-

All born from a bang.

Celestial bodies

Align in cosmic wonder-

Sparkling in the sky

Through time we travel,

A journey beyond measure,

Past and future merge

Whispers of the wind

Cast a spell with a flicker;

Magic's in the air.

Heavy clouds above,

Lonely heart and troubled mind,

Hope for sun to shine

Wandering the world,

Paths and roads unknown to me,

Adventures await.

Nervous silence looms,

Words fail to break the tension,

Awkward date unfolds.

Positive, negative

Vibes surround us every day

Choose to feel the light

Be you; unapologetic

Embrace all that makes you unique

Find joy in being true

Go live your best life

Shake what your mama gave ya

Like no one's watching

Miles away in space;

But your essence still lingers

Like a warm embrace

Glitter jumpsuit on

I'm feeling myself tonight.

Getting my groove back

Take a deep breath now

Sometimes it's one of those days-

Not today, Satan.

I'm doing my best

Just to get through the day;

Jesus take the wheel

Strangers in the void

How distant you feel from me,

Although you're right here.

Is tonight the night?

Right energy, wrong person –

Bad choices linger

Caressed by the sun

Embraced like a warm cuddle,

Sunbathed in solace

The things I've whispered

Secretly into the winds

While no one's watching

Toxic mind circles

Never-ending carousel

Dizzy from this ride

Will he or won't he?

The never-ending question

Of a gas-lit love

Tennis game of love

A never-ending gameplay

Still stuck at 0.

Players gonna play

And the haters gonna hate

But I stay winning

Stop acting up fool

Before I turn you into-

A revenge haiku

Random thoughts confined

All into 3 little lines –

Orbiting my mind

Fuck my life right now

The D appointment cancelled

New one on the way

How lonely it feels;

You're sitting right next to me

But feel worlds away.

Please stop texting me

I barely even know you

Delete my number

Well, this was awkward...

I got to go now see ya!

Uber on the way